AN INVITATION TO THE
BUTTERFLY BALL

A Counting Rhyme

By Jane Yolen

Illustrations by Jane Breskin Zalben

PHILOMEL BOOKS
New York

Text copyright © 1976 by Jane Yolen
Illustrations copyright © 1976 by Jane Breskin Zalben
First published in hardcover by
Parents Magazine Press, 1976.
Published in paperback in 1983 by Philomel Books,
a division of The Putnam Publishing Group,
51 Madison Avenue, New York, N.Y. 10010.
Printed in the United States of America.

Library of Congress Cataloging in Publication Data
Yolen, Jane.   An invitation to the butterfly ball.
   Reprint. Originally published: New York: Parents
Magazine Press, 1976.
   Summary: All the invited animals, from one little
mouse to ten little porcupines, busily prepare to
attend the Butterfly Ball.
   [1. Counting-out rhymes.   2. Animals — Fiction]
I. Zalben, Jane Breskin, ill.   II. Title.
PZ8.2.Y76In 1983   [E]   82-22462
ISBN 0-399-20972-7 (pbk.)

for
1. *little Heidi*
2. *little Adam*
3. *little Jason*

and
4. *Marvin Bileck,*
   a big elf who is so special

AN INVITATION TO THE
BUTTERFLY BALL

Knock. Knock. Who's come to call?
An invitation to the Butterfly Ball.

ONE little mouse in great distress
Looks all over for a floor-length dress.
"If I can't find one smaller than small,
Then I can't go to the Butterfly Ball."

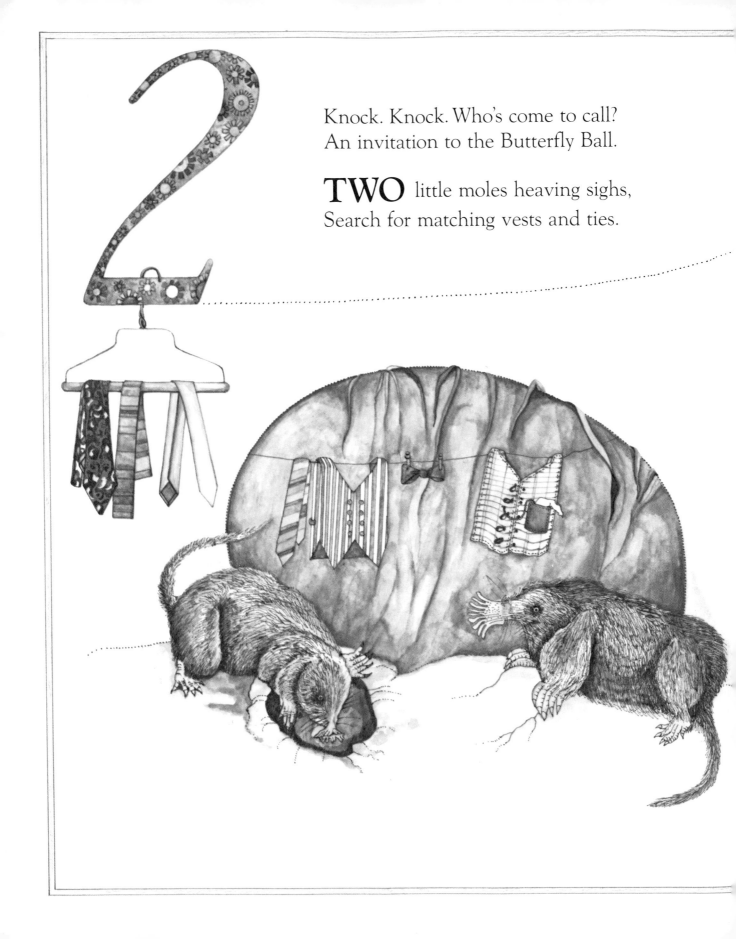

Knock. Knock. Who's come to call?
An invitation to the Butterfly Ball.

TWO little moles heaving sighs,
Search for matching vests and ties.

One little mouse in great distress
Looks all over for a floor-length dress.
If she can't find one smaller than small,
Then she can't go to the Butterfly Ball.

Knock. Knock. Who's come to call?
An invitation to the Butterfly Ball.

THREE little rabbits with very sad faces
Sort out their ribbons and baubles and laces.
Two little moles heaving sighs,
Search for matching vests and ties.

One little mouse in great distress
Looks all over for a floor-length dress.
If she can't find one smaller than small,
Then she can't go to the Butterfly Ball.

Knock. Knock. Who's come to call?
An invitation to the Butterfly Ball.

FOUR little skunks in a loud dispute,
Each one clamors for the one clean suit.
Three little rabbits with very sad faces
Sort out their ribbons and baubles and laces.
Two little moles heaving sighs,
Search for matching vests and ties.

One little mouse in great distress
Looks all over for a floor-length dress.
If she can't find one smaller than small,
Then she can't go to the Butterfly Ball.

Knock. Knock. Who's come to call?
An invitation to the Butterfly Ball.

FIVE little turtles wringing their flippers
Seek out dainty party slippers.
Four little skunks in a loud dispute,
Each one clamors for the one clean suit.
Three little rabbits with very sad faces
Sort out their ribbons and baubles and laces.
Two little moles heaving sighs,
Search for matching vests and ties.

One little mouse in great distress
Looks all over for a floor-length dress.
If she can't find one smaller than small,
Then she can't go to the Butterfly Ball.

Knock. Knock. Who's come to call?
An invitation to the Butterfly Ball.

SIX little owls with mournful hoots
Long for sleek black dancing boots.
Five little turtles wringing their flippers
Seek out dainty party slippers.
Four little skunks in a loud dispute,
Each one clamors for the one clean suit.
Three little rabbits with very sad faces
Sort out their ribbons and baubles and laces.
Two little moles heaving sighs,
Search for matching vests and ties.

One little mouse in great distress
Looks all over for a floor-length dress.
If she can't find one smaller than small,
Then she can't go to the Butterfly Ball.

Knock. Knock. Who's come to call?
An invitation to the Butterfly Ball.

SEVEN little raccoons send up wails.
They cannot find their silken veils.

Six little owls with mournful hoots
Long for sleek black dancing boots.
Five little turtles wringing their flippers
Seek out dainty party slippers.
Four little skunks in a loud dispute,
Each one clamors for the one clean suit.
Three little rabbits with very sad faces
Sort out their ribbons and baubles and laces.
Two little moles heaving sighs,
Search for matching vests and ties.

One little mouse in great distress
Looks all over for a floor-length dress.
If she can't find one smaller than small,
Then she can't go to the Butterfly Ball.

Knock. Knock. Who's come to call?
An invitation to the Butterfly Ball.

EIGHT little foxes in a terrible flap,
Each one hunting for a fine wool cap.
Seven little raccoons send up wails.
They cannot find their silken veils.
Six little owls with mournful hoots
Long for sleek black dancing boots.
Five little turtles wringing their flippers
Seek out dainty party slippers.
Four little skunks in a loud dispute,
Each one clamors for the one clean suit.
Three little rabbits with very sad faces
Sort out their ribbons and baubles and laces.
Two little moles heaving sighs,
Search for matching vests and ties.

One little mouse in great distress
Looks all over for a floor-length dress.
If she can't find one smaller than small,
Then she can't go to the Butterfly Ball.

Knock. Knock. Who's come to call?
An invitation to the Butterfly Ball.

NINE little frogs with dull hoarse croaks
Call for crimson evening cloaks.
Eight little foxes in a terrible flap,
Each one hunting for a fine wool cap.
Seven little raccoons send up wails.
They cannot find their silken veils.
Six little owls with mournful hoots
Long for sleek black dancing boots.
Five little turtles wringing their flippers
Seek out dainty party slippers.
Four little skunks in a loud dispute,
Each one clamors for the one clean suit.
Three little rabbits with very sad faces
Sort out their ribbons and baubles and laces.
Two little moles heaving sighs,
Search for matching vests and ties.

One little mouse in great distress
Looks all over for a floor-length dress.
If she can't find one smaller than small,
Then she can't go to the Butterfly Ball.

Knock. Knock. Who's come to call?
An invitation to the Butterfly Ball.
TEN little porcupines set up a racket,
As they fight for the velvet evening jacket.
Nine little frogs with dull hoarse croaks
Call for crimson evening cloaks.
Eight little foxes in a terrible flap,
Each one hunting for a fine wool cap.
Seven little raccoons send up wails.
They cannot find their silken veils.
Six little owls with mournful hoots
Long for sleek black dancing boots.

Five little turtles wringing their flippers
Seek out dainty party slippers.
Four little skunks in a loud dispute,
Each one clamors for the one clean suit.
Three little rabbits with very sad faces
Sort out their ribbons and baubles and laces.
Two little moles heaving sighs,
Search for matching vests and ties.

One little mouse in great distress
Looks all over for a floor-length dress.
If she can't find one smaller than small,
Then she can't go to the Butterfly Ball.

"Silken veils!"   "Sleek black boots!"

"A jacket!"

"Evening cloaks!"

"Fine wool caps!"

"Dainty Slippers!"

"A tiny, perfect floor-length dress!"

"Ribbons! Baubles! Laces!"

"A clean suit!"

"Matching vests and ties!"

"We have found them all!
Now we can go to the Butterfly Ball."

Knock. Knock...Who's come to call?

WE HAVE!!
We've *all* come to the Butterfly Ball.

Jane Yolen is the author of over fifty distinguished books for children, including poetry, stories, novels, and informational books. Many of her tales have won critical acclaim, including a Lewis Carroll Shelf Award, a Caldecott Honorable Mention, and a National Book Award nomination. "A storyteller from a long line of storytellers," Ms. Yolen lives with her husband, who is also a writer, and their three children in a big old farmhouse in western Massachusetts. She and Jane Breskin Zalben have also collaborated on All in the Woodland Early: An ABC Book.

Jane Breskin Zalben is a well-known illustrator of children's books, a painter, etcher, and book designer. Her beautiful illustrations for Lewis Carroll's Jabberwocky have brought her particular acclaim. She also writes many of the books she illustrates, including the recently published Porcupine's Christmas Blues. Ms. Zalben is on the faculty of the School of Visual Arts in New York City. She lives in Port Washington, New York, with her husband, an architect, and their two small children.

This text was set in Goudy Old Style and the display type
in Goudy Handtooled. The book was designed by Jane Zalben
and Mildred Kantrowitz.